GROUP PROCESSES

AN INTRODUCTION
TO GROUP DYNAMICS

JOSEPH LUFT, Ph.D.

Psychology Division
San Francisco State College

Lecturer, Medical Center
University of California

"What was so shocking in Galileo's astronomical discoveries? That there was so much going on in the sky and the astronomical order was so much less definite than one could happily believe before." W. Kohler (28)

NATIONAL PRESS BOOKS
850 HANSEN WAY
PALO ALTO, CALIFORNIA 94304

The field of group dynamics, group processes, is a roughly defined area in the social sciences. It overlaps disciplines such as social psychology, sociology, psychiatry, industrial psychology, social work, and clinical psychology. Contributions come from applied and theoretical fields, from practical problems of everyday life to highly specialized theoretical issues; from the intuitions of researchers and psychoanalysts to the practical experiences of industrial managers, from work with families to conceptions of mathematical models of communication, from the observations of children at play to the reports of councils of nations.

The subject matter of group dynamics is nowhere clearly organized. It continues to grow and sprout in all directions. Much of the knowledge is tentative and many of the theories are spotty and inadequate. Indeed, the field itself is so controversial that some legitimate investigators are wary of associating themselves with the name for fear questions be raised about their reputations as scholars. But then, the history of science informs us of similar fears and problems in astronomy, physics, medicine, psychoanalysis, and many other disciplines which are today well established. Philosophers of science tell us that knowledge begins with problems. If that is so, then the study of people in face-to-face groups is pre-eminently qualified as a field for scientific inquiry. Perhaps it has always been a principal concern of thoughtful men in every era. But today the need to learn about human behavior in groups is greater and more urgent than at any other time since the beginnings of human society.

Contents

What is group dynamics?

Why is the laboratory method used to teach group dynamics?

What are the basic issues in group dynamics?

These three questions will serve as a guide in this outline of group dynamics. In an academic field which is growing so rapidly, any attempt to summarize the work will necessarily be selective and will reflect the point of view and the biases of the writer. Furthermore, this syllabus will emphasize the learning and teaching of group dynamics rather than focusing on industrial, educational, or experimental aspects of the field.

The term "group dynamics" usually refers to the study of individuals interacting in small groups. The word "dynamics" implies forces which are complex and interdependent in a common field or setting. Unfortunately, there is no precise meaning in vogue today, so that beyond the brief definition given here it is necessary to determine any special meaning by examining the particular sense in which it is used. Because of the vagueness of the term, it is probably best to avoid using the expression except in a general way to indicate the broad field. As a matter of fact, the term itself is in some disrepute because it is sometimes used to convey rather unclear or mystical entities. Substitute terms have appeared, such as group processes, group psychology, and human relations, but no one appears to be entirely satisfied.

Group dynamics is most closely associated with field theory in contemporary psychology. Kurt Lewin, who organized and developed field theory,* is generally considered to be the

---

*Field theory, as defined by Lewin, is not a theory in the usual sense, but "a method of analyzing causal relations and of building scientific constructs." It is closely related to Gestalt theory, especially as regards the interdependence of part-whole relationships in behavior and experience. Some basic field theoretical constructs include (a) life space--all the facts that have existence for the individual or group at a particular time; (b) tension, energy, need, valence, and vector are dynamic concepts essential to the analysis of behavior; (c) processes such as perceiving, thinking, feeling, acting, and remembering are the means by which tensions in a system become equalized; (d) learning refers to a variety of processes involving change, such as a change in cognitive structure (new knowledge), change in motivation (learning new likes or dislikes), or change in group belongingness, as in growing into a culture (32).

founder of modern group dynamics. His work at the University
of Iowa in the mid-1930's, and later at the Massachusetts Institute of Technology, firmly established group dynamics in the
academic world and opened exciting new problems and methods
for psychologists, sociologists, educators, and other social
scientists. Articles and books by Lewin, such as Frontiers in
Group Dynamics (32), Group Decision and Social Change (30),
Dynamic Theory of Personality, and Resolving Social Conflicts
(30), paved the way for the postwar flood of investigations and
publications.

A decade later, Crutchfield (18), reviewing research in social
psychology and group processes, found that, "The frontier field
of group dynamics shows perhaps the greatest upsurge of all,
with its convincing demonstrations of how crucial psychological variables can be dealt with experimentally in a genuine
group setting."

One important finding by Lewin and his associates has a direct bearing on the second question at the head of this syllabus:
Why is the laboratory method used to teach group dynamics?
Lewin reported experiments aimed at teaching people such
things as changing food patterns or increasing work production
during the war. He found that certain methods of group discussion and decision were superior to lecturing and individual
instruction for changing ideas and social conduct. Eventually,
these group methods were applied to the learning of group
dynamics itself as a field of knowledge and as an applied skill.
Giving people information about food does not result in changes
in food preferences, because personal attitudes remain unaffected by the mere presentation of facts. Similarly, very little
seems to be learned by telling people about interpersonal behavior in groups, because personal attitudes and behavior are
unaffected. However, given an opportunity to work in a laboratory group, most people become sufficiently involved so that
they can feel and observe the processes while learning to con-
ceptualize them. In this way, participants learn something
about their own behavior in groups and develop insights into
group dynamics in general. A teacher of group processes
finds repeatedly that students usually get very little out of the
assigned readings in the field unless they can relate the text-
book ideas to their immediate experience. As the course moves
on, students report spontaneously that the readings suddenly
begin to have more meaning and are much more interesting
than they initially seemed. The various laboratories in group
dynamics tend to confirm these impressions.

Lewin's findings were supported by a number of investigators

NB ✓

working in diverse settings. Coch and French (14), for example, explored the reasons underlying resistance to changing methods of manufacturing textiles in a Virginia factory with 600 employees. They found that, "Change can be accomplished by the use of group meetings in which management effectively communicates the need for change and stimulates group participation in planning the changes." In another instance, researchers compared the effectiveness of the lecture method versus group decision in changing behavior of 395 workers and 29 supervisors in a large manufacturing plant. In their results these investigators state, "Our findings completely confirm those of Lewin in demonstrating the greater effectiveness of group decision over the lecture method of training." (29) Supervisors using the discussion group decision method learned about their tendency to overrate the work of skilled workers while downgrading the results of the less skilled workers. They were then better able to rate employees more in line with what a worker did, rather than with what prestige or rank the employee held. The supervisors learned about their biases and were able to do something about them as a result of group discussion, but not as a result of the lecture method.

The value of group discussion as compared to lecture method in the study of psychology has been demonstrated in a number of reports. (41) The results generally show that in both methods students learn about the same amount of subject matter of psychology. However, as reported by McKeachie (40), the group-centered class develops greater insight into personality dynamics than does the straight lecture class. They seem better able to apply what they learn to new problems. It should be mentioned that the results pertaining to teaching methods in psychology are not conclusive by any means, with individual differences in the values and the skill of the instructor as important variables.

The National Training Laboratory specializing in informal, experimental methods for teaching group dynamics was formed at Bethel, Maine, in 1947. Since its inception, N.T.L. has brought together specialists in the fields of psychology, sociology, education, industrial relations, anthropology, psychiatry, and philosophy to examine critically the problems of group dynamics and the methods employed to teach the subject. One of the unique aspects of the study of small groups is that it is still an interdisciplinary field of knowledge. The laboratory method continued to evolve by trial and error as well as by controlled experimentation, so that today N.T.L. is a firmly established educational institution and dozens of similar laboratories have sprung up at colleges and universities across the country. Research and self-criticism by the various staffs continue without letup, even though the laboratory method for teaching group dynamics has clearly proven its effectiveness.

Indeed, these methods have spread beyond the limits of the academic world into fields as diverse as industrial and educational management, public health, mental hygiene, medicine, labor organization, public personnel administration, and business enterprises. Many non-academic people are, of course, continually faced by problems of group dynamics--whether or not they are aware of this field. For example, one engineer wants to know how to improve the effectiveness of his staff; he knows he has hired capable men but for some reason they seem unable to work together. A school administrator cannot understand why his teachers are constantly feuding, even though their salaries and working conditions are identical with those in other schools nearby which do not have these problems. Executives are concerned about the training of young managers, and are at a loss to know how leadership can be taught.

These are not unusual problems by any means and increasing numbers are taking advantage of the workshops by N.T.L. and university programs around the country. Some of the colleges present these laboratories through their extension services. Others offer the lab from time to time. The Tavistock Institute of Human Relations in England is probably the most important center for teaching group processes in Europe.

The program at Michigan has been described by Lippitt (36) as follows: "The University of Michigan at its Research Center for Group Dynamics in its broad program is attempting to study small groups experimentally, to seek integration with work in related social science fields, and to apply findings to such socially useful activity as supervisor training, group therapy, etc. The work done includes studies of communities, factory work groups, discussion groups, leadership groups in training, and other face-to-face groups."

It hardly seems necessary to state that it is important to study how groups function. Still, it is true that many people are opposed to the whole idea of group dynamics. Articles and books have been written to criticize the field and to discredit the findings. Some writers are so opposed to group efforts of any kind, that to recognize the mere existence of groups is tantamount to advocating more extensive use of groups. Some critics believe that the group dynamics specialists are overstating the claims of the work done in the field, or they criticize the paucity of controlled research. Still others consider the whole movement a mere fad or cult which will fade away just as phrenology and Coue-ism did. And then, there are persons who consider the field as dangerous for society because they feel it will teach people how to manipulate or exploit others. (6)

But groups do exist, in homes and schools, in business and professions, in government and military life. For the scientist, any natural or social phenomenon is an appropriate subject for study. It seems strange to need to affirm this in the twentieth century. Groups exist, and it is a legitimate scientific assumption that rigorous inquiry will yield principles governing the orderliness of group processes. The more important question to raise on this score is: Will scientific method be employed so that others may be able to check the validity and reliability of results? The twin hazards, cultism and anti-intellectualism, from within the field and from outside, are best avoided by open discussion and by the sharing of ideas and data in the scientific tradition.

And as far as the possible misuse of knowledge is concerned, there is little we can do short of some kind of thought control (censorship), which few would care to advocate. Every human advance since the invention of the wheel could potentially be used against people, against society. Working and living in groups present so many problems and difficulties that to neglect to inquire how people live and function in groups would incur even more serious risks than those arising out of the possible abuse of knowledge in this field.

In his discussion of research on groups and leadership, Lewin (31) notes the value as well as the hazards for the behavioral scientist: "It would be most unfortunate if the trend toward theoretical psychology were weakened by the necessity of dealing with natural groups when studying certain problems of social psychology. One should not be blind, however, to the fact that this development offers great opportunities as well as threats to theoretical psychology. The greatest handicap of applied psychology has been the fact that, without proper theoretical help, it had to follow the costly, inefficient, and limited method of trial and error. Many psychologists working today in an applied field are keenly aware of the need for close cooperation between theoretical and applied psychology. This can be accomplished in psychology, as it has been accomplished in physics, if the theorist does not look toward applied problems with highbrow aversion or with a fear for social problems, and if the applied psychologist realizes that there is nothing as practical as a good theory. In the field of group dynamics, more than in any other psychological field, theory and practice are linked methodologically in a

way which, if properly handled, could provide answers to theoretical problems and at the same time strengthen that rational
approach to our practical social problems which is one of the
basic requirements for their solution." (33)

Reprinted by permission of United Features Syndicate and The San Francisco Chronicle.

Formal conventional ways of studying groups are minimized.
Although lectures may be given and textbooks recommended,
they constitute supplementary parts of the program. Schedules
are arranged so that the group members know when and where
to meet, but no subject matter guide is used. Each collection
of people studying group dynamics is challenged to find its own
way through the subject matter, using the resources of its own
group participants. Meetings usually last from one and one-
half to two hours.

The physical arrangement of the class is more like a seminar
or workshop. There is no head of the class or fixed seats. This
arrangement is proposed in order to facilitate free discussion
within the group. In addition, it encourages independent member
initiative instead of the usual reliance on the teacher at the head
of the class.

Removing the study group from the usual surroundings and the
usual social pressures is advocated by some laboratories. The
idea of a "cultural island" has many advantages. By freeing the
individual from his customary work set, it tends to encourage a
fresh look at familiar problems. There is more time to think
these matters over and to discuss them in pleasant surroundings with others who are equally interested. Although such a
setting is preferred, it is not always possible for practical
reasons.

The newly formed group in the laboratory is encouraged to
leave behind the usual symbols and trappings of status. Dress
is usually quite informal; titles are omitted, so that people are
addressed simply as "mister" instead of "doctor" or "professor."
Sometimes, members choose to use first names, but this is, of
course, a matter of individual preference.

Although the instructor has some special functions and responsibilities, he participates as a member of the group and encourages other members to participate as freely as possible and in
whatever way they can. The instructor assumes a more passive
role than is usually the case in college classes. There are
many important reasons for this. Since the group is new and has
never before worked together, the instructor avoids imposing a
pattern of work which may not spring from the unique characteristics of this particular collection of persons. Also, the members are immediately faced with the problem of finding their
own way of proceeding in the group. Thus, important issues,
such as the setting of short-range and long-range goals, the
establishment of ways and means of working on problems, the

nature of its own communication system and decision-making
processes--these and many more problems must somehow be
faced and resolved. It is in the struggle with these issues that
the basis for learning about group and individual behavior is
grounded.

 The content of group discussions and the processes underlying group behavior are distinguished and clarified. The word
"process" refers to an inference made about the meaning of
behavior in the group. Behavior may be verbal, as in discussion,
or non-verbal, as in keeping silent or facing a particular person
while addressing the group. There is an unlimited variety of
group processes, some of which are commonly used and easily
understood. For example, some group members may become
involved in matters which take the group away from its immediate work, yet most of the group will go along with this detour,
and only later will the members recognize the real need to temporarily escape the task at hand. Such detours or flights from
the necessary work of the group are important processes, and
probably constitute one of the universal properties of all groups.
Lewin makes a similar distinction, using the terms "phenotype"
and "genotype." A phenotype refers to observable behavior,
that which is said or done. A genotype is an idea or construct
about the underlying meaning of behavior.

 The laboratory method requires a permissive atmosphere.
Participants recognize after a while that they are freer to ask,
to challenge, to question, to contribute, to listen, and to explore.
Members discover that they can be themselves more, to say
what they really think, or to express attitudes which they would
ordinarily disguise or ignore. After a cautious beginning, and
after testing the "temperature of the atmosphere," members
find it increasingly valuable to be able to check their impressions with others, to admit that they do not understand something when they really do not, or to participate in new ways
which they may never have permitted themselves. An atmosphere free of the usual psychological threat is most conducive
to learning about one's own role in a group.

 One of the reasons for relying on such informal discussion
methods for learning about groups is that in his experience
within the group, the learner discovers how closely and com-
plexly related are the various processes of group life. It is one
thing to talk or read about how groups make decisions, but it is
quite another matter when he participates with his peers and
struggles through to a decision. Here he can see, for instance,
that decisions of the group may be influenced by overt as well

phenotype

genotype

as by covert conflicts in the group, by communication problems, by the status of members acquired while in the group, by sensitive conciliators as well as by information suppliers and by passive supporters.

The laboratory method makes it possible to discover certain phases in the development of the group. Frequently, many groups find through their own experience that initial progress in the group was accomplished at the expense of certain members. The progress may or may not be substantial, but it takes a while to find out that the member who has been bypassed, or squelched in his efforts, may resent the progress made and consequently may withdraw from active participation without being quite aware of it. Or he may retaliate at another time when the group least expects it. At any rate, hasty progress made in this way may boomerang, so that the group loses much more than it gains when a premature solution is made. When the group members are sufficiently free of anxiety to point out what has happened, when they have become as much interested in the way progress is made as well as in the progress itself, that eventually the group moves in the direction of more effective decisions. Such decisions may then reflect the knowledge and skills of its members as well as their motives and feelings. That these earlier and later phases do exist is indicated by the fact that premature decisions are rarely given the support they need, while later, more considered actions, tempered by conflicts and their resolution, are followed through to conclusion.

Finally, the laboratory method is preferred because many persons are as much interested in improving their own ability to work in a group as they are in learning about groups. In the belief that the two objectives complement each other, the laboratory offers many opportunities to become more aware of one's own behavior and the behavior of others. In a group, one can check what he knows about behavior with behavior as it actually is. And each member is encouraged to explore and to find new and more effective ways of working with others. As a participant-observer, each member can find out for himself whether his explicit values about people coincide with his behavior toward them.

The mark of a civilized man is his willingness to reexamine his most cherished beliefs.   Oliver Wendell Holmes

Chapter III
The Johari Window
A Graphic Model of Awareness
In Interpersonal Relations

Like the happy centipede, many people get along fine working
with others without thinking about which foot to put forward.
But when there are difficulties, when the usual methods do not
work, when we want to learn more--there is no alternative but
to examine our own behavior in relation to others. The trouble
is, among other things, it is so hard to find ways of thinking
about such matters, particularly for people who have no extensive backgrounds in the social sciences.

When Ingham and Luft (38) first presented "The Johari Window"
to illustrate relationships in terms of awareness, they were surprised to find so many people, academicians and non-profes-
sionals alike, using, and tinkering with, the model. It seems to
lend itself as a heuristic device, to speculating about human
relations. It is simple to visualize the four quadrants which
represent the Johari Window:

	Known to Self	Not Known to Self
Known to Others	I Area of Free Activity	II Blind Area
Not Known to Others	III Avoided or Hidden Area	IV Area of Unknown Activity

Figure A.   The Johari Window

10

Quadrant I, the Area of Free Activity, refers to behavior and motivation known to self and known to others.

Quadrant II, the Blind Area, where others can see things in ourselves of which we are unaware.

Quadrant III, the Avoided or Hidden Area, represents things we know but do not reveal to others (e.g., a hidden agenda, or matters about which we have sensitive feelings).

Quadrant IV, Area of Unknown Activity. Neither the individual nor others are aware of certain behaviors or motives. Yet, we can assume their existence because eventually some of these things become known, and it is then realized that these unknown behaviors and motives were influencing relationships all along. _NB_

In a new group, Quadrant I is very small; there is not much free and spontaneous interaction. As the group grows and matures, Quadrant I expands in size, and this usually means we are freer to be more like ourselves and to perceive others as they really are. Quadrant III shrinks in area as Quadrant I grows larger. We find it less necessary to hide or deny things we know or feel. In an atmosphere of growing mutual trust, there is less need for hiding pertinent thoughts or feelings. It takes longer for Quadrant II to reduce in size, because usually there are "good" reasons of a psychological nature to blind ourselves to the things we feel or do. Quadrant IV changes somewhat during a learning laboratory, but we can assume that such changes occur even more slowly than shifts in Quadrant II. At any rate, Quadrant IV is undoubtedly far larger and more influential in an individual's relationships than the hypothetical sketch illustrates.

The Johari Window may be applied to intergroup relations. Quadrant I means behavior and motivation known to the group, and also known to other groups. Quadrant II signifies an area of behavior to which a group is blind, but other groups are aware of this behavior, e.g., cultism or prejudice. Quadrant III, the hidden area, refers to things a group knows about itself, but which is kept from other groups. Quadrant IV, the unknown area, means a group is unaware of some aspects of its own behavior, and other groups are also unaware of this behavior. Later, as the group learns new things about itself, there is a shift from Quadrant IV to one of the other quadrants.

PRINCIPLES OF CHANGE

a. A change in any one quadrant will affect all other quadrants.
b. It takes energy to hide, deny, or be blind to behavior which is involved in interaction.

c. Threat tends to decrease awareness; mutual trust tends to increase awareness.

d. Forced awareness (exposure) is undesirable and usually ineffective.

e. Interpersonal learning means a change has taken place so that Quadrant I is larger, and one or more of the other quadrants has grown smaller.

f. Working with others is facilitated by a large enough area of free activity. It means more of the resources and skills in the membership can be applied to the task at hand.

g. The smaller the first quadrant, the poorer the communication.

h. There is universal curiosity about the unknown area; but this is held in check by custom, social training, and by diverse fears.

i. Sensitivity means appreciating the covert aspects of behavior, in Quadrants II, III, IV, and respecting the desire of others to keep them so.

j. Learning about group processes, as they are being experienced, helps to increase awareness (larger Quadrant I) for the group as a whole as well as for individual members.

k. The value system of a group and its membership may be noted in the way unknowns in the life of the group are confronted.

l. A centipede may be perfectly happy without awareness· but after all, he restricts himself to crawling under rocks.

Having familiarized himself with this outline, each group member might learn to use it to help himself to a clearer understanding of the significant events in a group. Furthermore the plan is sufficiently broad and loose so that it may have heuristic value in stimulating the identification and elaboration of problems in new ways. Several illustrations of different kinds of intergroup and intragroup behavior are given here.

The Objectives of a Group Dynamics Laboratory

Using this model, we may illustrate one of the general objectives of the laboratory, namely, to increase the area of free activity in Quadrant I so that more of the relationships in the group are free and open. It follows, therefore, that the work of the laboratory is to increase the area of Quadrant I while reducing the area of Quadrants II, III and IV. The largest reduction in area would be in Quadrant III, then Quadrant II and the smallest reduction in Quadrant IV.

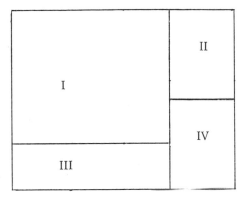

Figure B. Laboratory objectives.

An enlarged area of free activity among the group members would immediately imply less threat or fear and greater probability that the skills and resources of group members could be brought to bear on the work of the group. It suggests greater openness to information, opinions and new ideas about oneself as well as about specific group processes. Since the hidden or avoided area, Quadrant III, is reduced, it implies that less energy is tied up in defending this area. Since more of one's needs are unbound, there is greater likelihood of satisfaction with the work, and more involvement with what the group is doing.

The Initial Phase of Group Interaction

Applying the model to a typical meeting of most groups, we can recognize that interaction is relatively superficial, that anxiety

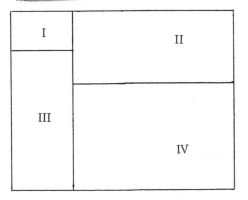

Figure C. Beginning interaction in a new group.

or threat is fairly large, that interchange is stilted and unspon-
taneous. We also may note that ideas or suggestions are not
followed through and are usually left undeveloped, that individuals
seem to hear and see relatively little of what is really going on.

The Model May Depict Intergroup Processes as Well as Intragroup Processes

The group may be treated as an entity or unit. Cattell (11),
for instance, uses the term "syntality" to mean the quality of a
group analogous to the personality of an individual. Lewin con-
ceives of the group as an organized field of forces, a structured
whole. In this model, a group may relate to other groups in a
manner similar to the relationship between individuals. For instance, in Figure D, the first quadrant represents behavior and
motivation of a group which is known to group members and also
known to others. A college seminar, for instance, may share
certain knowledge and behavior about itself with other classes
on campus, such as requirements for the course, subject matter
of the seminar, or the amount of work it sets out to do. However,
many things occur in a seminar that are known to its members,
but not known to outside groups (Quadrant III).

	Known to Group	Not Known to Group
Known to Other Groups	I	II
Not Known to Other Groups	III	IV

Figure D. Interaction between groups.

An illustration of an area of avoided behavior might be the feeling that their seminar is very special or quite superior to other
classes. Or they might feel the course is a waste of time, but
for some reason they do not share this attitude with outsiders.
Or sometimes a special event occurs, and this is kept from outsiders. Quadrant II, the blind area, is characteristic of certain

cults which are unaware of some aspects of their own behavior while outsiders seem able to discern the cultish qualities. Or, sometimes, the prejudices of a group may be perfectly apparent to outsiders but not to the group members themselves.

Quadrant IV might apply to attitudes and behavior which exist in the group but for some reason remain unknown to the group. An illustration of this might be an unresolved problem with regards to over-all goals of the group. If the group is covertly split and some members want to go off in different directions-- and if this fact has never been recognized or brought out in the open--then we could see the development of difficulties which remain unknown to the group members and unknown to the members of other groups. For example, in a large scientific enterprise, the physicists and engineers were having great difficulty with the machinists. Only after a long period of investigation did it become apparent that the question of status and privilege was producing bitter feelings between groups, yet the members of the various groups were unaware of the ramification of this problem.

Reprinted by permission of United Features Syndicate and The San Francisco Chronicle.

There are so many important issues bearing on the study of
groups that only a limited number will be touched on here. Most
of the large issues, such as communication, leadership, cooperation, and competition, are so vast as to require separate courses
and texts at the college level. References at the end of the syllabus will offer the student leads for further reading. Selected and
discussed in this chapter is a series of topics particularly germane to a laboratory approach to group processes. It will be
noted that comments on one topic invariably bring in other issues.
The division of group behavior into different segments and processes is an artificial dissection of an integrated whole, for purposes of simplification and discussion.

Process and Content

When a group assembles to do a particular job, such as working out a new budget or learning about physics, the members
concern themselves primarily with content, the literal task or
subject matter. However, difficulties may emerge in the group
which have no direct relation to the budget or to physics. There
may develop problems in communication even though the language
is clear, or harsh feelings may develop between the instructor
and students, or the committee may bog down in fruitless squab-
bles between factions. These indirect problems involve processes, and require recognition and special attention if the group
is to get on with its work. In a group dynamics laboratory, the
distinction between the two levels of functioning is clarified and
various approaches are presented to show how processes can be
constructively identified. The participant-observer learns to
consider these processes in a non-judgmental manner, so that
they may be understood without threatening the members.

Because many of the processes are subtle and difficult to identify, it is necessary to learn about them by experience and by
practice. All aspects of group activity may involve processes,
and each of the basic issues discussed in this section concern
themselves in one way or other with these underlying phenomena.
Structure, conflict, dependence-independence, role, and morale
are examples of ways of talking about processes.

Bion's Processes

A well-known system of processes was developed by British
psychiatrist Bion (9), who found these ideas useful beyond the

---

I have made a ceaseless effort not to ridicule, not to bewail, nor to scorn human
actions, but to understand them.   Spinoza

applications to group psychotherapy. He refers to the underlying emotional patterns of group life as "modalities." These may or may not interfere with the work of a group, but should be thought of as characterizing essential psychological processes. The fight-flight modality describes ways in which group members fight as a concomitant of work. Sometimes fighting occurs instead of group work because of inevitable differences in emotional needs. Fighting may be subtle and covert, or open and aggressive. Flight identifies the many different ways in which a group runs away or avoids the task for which they are organized. Pairing is another modality in which members join each other, often without being aware of it, in order to cope with problems or to increase personal satisfaction. Dependency is a modality which typifies a group seeking support from a person or a thing they see as stronger than themselves. Many other ways of systematizing group processes exist. For research purposes, investigators may develop their own system, or select certain processes for special attention. Operational definitions are desirable wherever possible, in order to avoid the hazards of subjective observation and interpretation.

Group Mind

Thirty or forty years ago, the question of group mind aroused strong controversy and criticism. The term was rejected as too vague and mystical. Today there is less resistance to the use of a construct pertaining to the group as a whole, provided that the same efforts at operational definition are made as is the case for other constructs such as intelligence or personality.

Lewin (30), for instance, talks about group atmosphere;* Cattell (11) uses the term "syntality" to describe the personality of the group; Cartwright (12) refers to the emotional dimensions of a group, the emotional tone of the group, and groups as healthy or pathological; Festinger (19), Libo (34), and others (3) write about group cohesiveness; Asch (1) and Crutchfield (17) examine group pressures and group conformity. These productive inquiries show that we need not fear using group relevant terms, for, as a matter of fact, if they did not exist, we would have to invent equivalents to serve as intervening variables in the building of adequate theories.

NB

---

*"It is well known that the amount of success a teacher has in the classroom depends not only on her skill but to a great extent on the atmosphere she creates. This atmosphere is something intangible; it is a property of the social situation as a whole, and may be measured scientifically if approached from this angle."

Dependence, Independence and Interdependence

Sherif (47) and, later, Asch (1), have shown experimentally how persons tend to yield their own judgment and depend on others, particularly when the situation is ambiguous. Asch's study is especially important, because he showed that even when the stimulus situation is not ambiguous, a significant number of persons will yield their independent judgment. Asch found that the estimation of length of lines against a standard line can easily be judged accurately when alone, but produces conflicts in a significant number of the subjects when others are present who deliberately give erroneous judgments. About one-third of the subjects yielded to the pressure exerted by the confederates of the experimenter and gave incorrect responses.

Many studies show how the independence-dependence-interdependence variables are related to other manifestations of group life. French (32) shows experimentally that organized (interdependent) groups are superior to unorganized groups in fear situations, by demonstrating greater social freedom and equality of participation under stress. Lewin, Lippitt and White (33) found that their experimental "democratic" groups of children were more independent and more interdependent than the "autocratic" groups. Seeman (46) notes that teachers oriented toward high status favor superintendents who would direct them more, and who would tell them what to do. Dependency and need for status seemed to go together.

If by independence we mean relying on one's own feelings, impressions, and judgment as a guide to action, and dependence means relying on others, then we must postulate interdependence as a significant process in a maturing group. Interdependence develops as a collection of individuals works out new procedures, standards and values appropriate to the goals and membership resources of the group. In addition to a division of labor within the group, interdependence means learning to accept dependence when realistically needed (as in a work team or in a bomber crew). The dependence shown in the experiments of Asch and Crutchfield was inappropriate to the problems confronted. In field theoretical terms, a group changes by restructuring the part-whole relationships into a new configuration. Changes in standards, roles, and patterns of communication influence the motivation of individuals as well as the group atmosphere. Lewin (31) calls this unfreezing, change of level or standards, and refreezing at a new level. Groups achieve interdependence through resolution of differences, so that cooperation and collaboration are optimal while independence of judgment and action are maximized.

Hemphill (23), in his leadership studies, finds that people

tolerate more leader-centered behavior in large groups than in
small, more personal groups. Also showing how the conditions
under which a group functions influences factors such as independence, Bavelas (5) experimented with group communication
network systems and found that dependency and leadership vary
with the network system. Crutchfield (17) extends Asch's
experiments using abstract as well as physical stimuli as a basis
of judgment, and finds that independence in thinking about ideas $N B$
is also readily yielded by significant proportions of individuals
when exposed to the misleading opinions of others. As in Asch's
experiment, the single individual had no opportunity to check his
impressions with others; there was no communication with the
dissenters.

Individual Versus Group Productivity

Is a group more effective at solving problems than individuals
working alone? A number of experiments on group versus individual effectiveness has failed to resolve this question. Kelley
and Thibaut (26) have summarized research on "Experimental
studies of group problem solving and process." Although research reports go back about thirty-five years, no systematic
principles have yet emerged.

It is obvious that many physical, structural, and process problems pertaining to groups are involved in this issue. Variables,
such as size of group, nature of task, composition of membership, time and quality factors, motivational forces from within
and from outside the group, imposed goals versus self-deter-
mined goals, intragroup communication, conformity pressures
and morale, and processes of interpersonal influences, have
been studied in scattered researches and have a direct bearing
on the question of productivity. But no comprehensive theory
has been developed to link these variables in a way which would
permit definitive answers. In a sense, the question of superior-
ity of individual as against group productivity is less important
than an understanding of what takes place when people work together. Even when we work alone, we are involved with the contributions of others; for example, the borrowing and lending of
ideas and techniques amongst scientists and artists. Also, our
present ability to work alone is a function of past learning.

Frequently, individual and group efforts supplement each other.
Executives and administrators need to know what other sectors
are doing--if only to avoid working at cross-purposes and dupli-
cation. A group effort is a necessary evil for some people, inhib-
iting and hampering freedom, reducing quality to mediocre levels.
But is this the inevitable result of group effort? The American
Declaration of Independence and the Constitution (52) are group

efforts; it is doubtful whether a single individual could have
done a superior job. On the other hand, how would a committee
have fared working, say, on the Moses sculpture by Michel-
angelo? Obviously the nature of the work is important as well
as personal preference.

A deeply integrated society with pluralistic aims calls for the
expression of diverse, individual needs, and for the resolution
of differences in the solution of certain problems. Planning a
new factory, changing the tax structure, or building a school
calls for broad awareness of needs and demands, and the advice
of the technical expert. Learning itself seems to progress best
for most people when there is an appropriate balance of learning
with others and studying alone. Unless we prefer a job (or a
society) which tells us what to do and how to do it, we are com-
mitted to a philosophy of interpersonal consultation. Within this
philosophy, however, there should be ample room for an optimal
balance between individual and group productivity. Perhaps an
enlightened self-interest can best guide us in deciding when a
group effort is required. And it is a wise group that knows when
to cease and expire.

Group Versus Individual Productivity--A Summary

a. There are definite advantages and disadvantages to group
   versus individual problem solving and productivity.
b. When a problem demands a single over-all insight, or an
   original set of decisions, an individual approach may be
   superior to a group effort.
c. Problems calling for a wide variety of skill and information,
   or the cross-checking of facts and ideas, seem to favor a
   group approach. Feedback and free exchange of thinking
   may actually stimulate ideas that would not have emerged
   by solo effort.
d. If goals are shared, then there is greater likelihood for
   cooperative effort; when the group goal is not shared by
   members, morale and productivity may suffer. Consequently, when the goal is decided upon by group discussion and
   participation, there is greater likelihood of full member
   involvement.
e. The greater the desire for individual prominence and distinction, the lower will be the friendly sharing or group
   morale.
f. Having decided on the need for group effort, the smaller the
   size of the group the better will it function, provided that
   the necessary diversity of skills and group maintenance
   resources are present.

g. A group may be a source of strong interpersonal stimulation; a group will also generate its own conformity pressures. In order to decide between group and individual work, these two sets of forces (stimulating and binding) should be kept in mind.

h. A society which places highest value on the worth and freedom of the individual also encourages strongest independent thought, independent work, and independent responsibility. An inherent goal of a sound group, therefore, is the reaffirmation of true independence while meeting group needs.

Structure

Structure refers to the internal organization and procedures of a group. All groups are faced with the problem of structure. ✓ It is not only a matter of how much structure, but whether the group will build its own rules, limits, and procedures appropriate to its own needs.

In an informal experiment at the National Training Laboratory at Bethel (49), homogeneous groups were arranged on the basis of need for structure by individual members. The high-structure group proceeded in a more direct and open manner, were more task oriented and less process oriented, seemed to move quickly toward surface communication and surface relationships, and showed greater deference to persons of power and authority. The low-structure group members were less concerned with task and more with process, were more supportive, and more interpretative of group and member feelings. One interesting observation concerned the lack felt by each group for qualities found in the other group. In other words, by screening out heterogeneous elements, the groups were deprived of the necessary balance between work and group maintenance roles.

Conflict

Many issues revolve around the meaning of conflict in group behavior. Is conflict essential for group productivity or creativity? Do groups blindly work their way through conflicts or can general processes be distinguished? Gordon Hearn (22) calls attention to Ewbank's contribution on this issue. Ewbank identifies five ways in which group conflicts are dealt with: first, eliminating the opposition; second, subjugating the opposition; third, forming an alliance to overpower the opposition; fourth, reaching a compromise with the other side; fifth, integrating opposing ideas toward new solutions. Conflict and consensus can be seen as powerful central issues in the dynamics of all groups.

ESOCI   CESoI

Thelen (51), Hearn (22) and others believe conflict is inevitable in all groups because the larger culture is continually struggling with issues such as competition versus cooperation, individuality versus conformity, freedom of expression versus inhibition of feelings.

Role

The concept of role means a pattern of behavior which characterizes an individual's place in a group. Cooley (16) was one of the first in contemporary sociology to point out the meaning and importance of group membership character. He stressed that one's role in different groups has a powerful bearing on the development of the individual, and that in his social behavior, multiple group membership is the key to understanding his motives. The concept of role may thus be helpful in the understanding and prediction of an individual's behavior. Sherif (48) and others have shown how multiple group identification may create problems for the individual and inconsistencies in his behavior. For example, a businessman may behave in a typically competitive role on his job, then he may act in a cooperative and supporting manner as a member of a church group. When faced with an issue such as school integration in his community, he may undergo considerable stress or act in an inconsistent manner with reference to this issue.

Similarly, in a small group it is possible to identify characteristic patterns of behavior for each of the members, and to relate these roles to the functioning of the group. Functional roles of group members are described by Benne and Sheats (8) as a way of cataloguing the task oriented activities. They use terms such as initiators, opinion or information givers and seekers, evaluators, recorders, etc., to describe behavior of group members concerned with the work of the group. Group building and group maintenance activities are described by another set of roles.

Bales (4) uses twelve broad categories of group behavior which are sufficiently descriptive to be usable for observation with some practice and training. To get at a more adequate description of role behavior, the following activities are listed on his interaction scoring form: 1. Shows solidarity, raises others' status, gives help, reward; 2. Shows tension release, jokes, laughs, shows satisfaction; 3. Agrees, shows passive acceptance, understands, concurs, complies; 4. Gives suggestion, direction, implying autonomy for others; 5. Gives opinion, evaluation, analysis, expresses feeling, wish; 6. Gives orientation, information, repeats, clarifies, confirms; 7. Asks for orientation, information, repetition, confirmation; 8. Asks for opinion,

evaluation, analysis, expression of feeling; 9. Asks for suggestion, direction, possible ways of action; 10. Disagrees, shows
passive rejection, formality, withholds help; 11. Shows tension,
asks for help, withdraws "out of field"; 12. Shows antagonism,
deflates others' status, defends or asserts self.

One of the interesting problems regarding roles is to identify
the principles underlying the changes in role of a group member.
Sociometric questionnaires may be used to learn how each member sees the other members and himself--at different stages in
the life of the group.

Role Playing

Role playing is a method for studying the attitudes and feelings
of individuals in simulated situations. For example, a supervisor may have traced some of his difficulties on the job to the
problem of employee evaluation. Under the direction of an experienced group leader, the supervisor is asked to reconstruct
a concrete problem situation. Group members are asked to take
different roles, with the supervisor participating or observing
others after he himself has participated. Then they improvise
dialogue and action to fit, roughly, the problem situation. In
spontaneous interaction of a play acting type, group members
may learn more about their own attitudes and behavior and try
to find new ways of dealing with their problems. Role playing
is usually followed by a free discussion of what went on and how
the actors and observers felt about the interactions. In this way,
productive new insights and ideas may be gained. Role playing
as a form of Psychodrama (42) is more complex than it seems,
and it would be unwise to apply it without the supervision of an
experienced person. Carried out by inexperienced people, role
playing may be misused and do more to arouse anxiety and to
confuse than it does to help people learn. Role playing may be
particularly valuable as a diagnostic device in controlled research situations.

Morale

For Lewin (32), morale means that a group's goals are
sufficiently high to reflect the ideals (or long-range goals) of
the group, but at the same time keeping in touch with reality for
work on immediate goals. Of the many meanings of morale,
the most common refers to the level of effectiveness of a group
and how the members feel about belonging to the group. It may
be described in terms of we-ness or solidarity feeling, or as
esprit-de-corps. A high morale group can endure greater conflicts and stress without serious damage, without falling apart.

Thus, there are two interrelated aspects to a group's morale: the extent to which an individual's personal needs are met, and the effectiveness with which the goals of the group are realized. But these two aspects do not always coincide.

Jennings (25) and Coffey (15) develop the idea that all groups are motivated by needs broadly subsumed under the terms "psyche" and "socio". For some group members, the characteristic mode of behaving is in terms of meeting their personal, emotional needs. Other members are less concerned with their emotional needs, or are less comfortable in dealing with feelings, and they may prefer to emphasize the socio or work aspects of group activity. Since all groups have both kinds of needs in varying degrees, it is necessary for each group to work out its most appropriate combination of these two components.

In the Western Electric study at Hawthorne, Illinois, Elton Mayo (39) and his associates were initially puzzled to find productivity rise even though certain physical conditions, such as lighting, were made less attractive. He later discovered that the morale of the small group under study rose due to certain social and personal factors, and consequently productivity continued to go up.

However, R. L. Kahn and Daniel Katz (13) found in their University of Michigan studies of leadership and morale, that there was no consistent relationship between morale and productivity in several different companies studied. They attribute this to the variations in ability of supervisors or to the fact that a cost-per-unit measure of productiveness was used, leaving out more intangible factors, such as reasons for absence and turnover on the job and scrap-loss in production.

In a laboratory on small groups, participants are exposed to the complexity of social and personal forces which have a bearing on morale, and can actually experience the fluctuation of morale in themselves and within the group. In describing the emergence of groupness out of conflicts, Hearn (22) found, in his seminars on group work process at the University of California, two issues on which the groups struggled. "The first was the problem of authority. Expressed in terms of ideological differences concerning the role of the instructor, it had to do with the issue of dependence versus independence. Each member struggled with this problem in his own way based, undoubtedly, upon his various experiences and reactions to authority in other settings. The other issue was expressed in questions concerning how much and what kind of structure was desirable in a group of this kind." Hearn found that his groups worked on these two issues throughout the entire course, as evidenced by

the process records which he wrote at the conclusion of each
class session. By tracing the genesis of these issues, Hearn
shows "how groupness emerges out of intermember conflict."

The meaning of morale is not yet adequately understood. One
thing is clear, however; most attempts to raise morale by
superficial means are bound to fail. When we understand that
individual satisfaction with one's group implies coming to terms
with the overt and covert motivational forces of both the members themselves and the group as a whole, we can begin to
appreciate how complex this is. When we recognize the large
individual differences which may exist among members of the
group, we can see support for the idea of maximum self-determination by the group. And, lastly, when we recognize that a
group may be part of a larger unit which exercises powerful
influence over the smaller group (as is true in industry, education, and government) we may understand better the range of
problems involved. For these reasons, there is currently a
trend in research to move away from the consideration of
morale as a single unitary problem, and to deal with significant
concomitants which are more readily controlled experimentally
and understood individually.

Communication

As with other basic processes such as role, conflict, structure,
and leadership, it is impossible to discuss communication without relating it to all phenomena of group life. Communication
refers to what is expressed verbally and non-verbally; it applies
to articulated words and thoughts, and to unvocalized feelings;
it concerns the intentions of the communicator and the impressions received by the ones to whom the communication is addressed. Communication may be formal as information con-
veyed in an organization through regular channels, or informal
as in the interactions among friends over coffee.

Difficulties in communication may result from real or imaginary threats to members of a group and must be related to questions of power and influence. Channels of communication may
be built into the structure of a group, as in industry or military
organizations, or channels may develop informally as a function
of interpersonal needs and conflicts. Sociometric assessment
may show, by means of friendship choices, where the informal
channels exist. Communication may increase toward deviate
members, and may cease altogether if the deviate moves too
far from the standards and norms of the group. The quality of
listening to others is of enormous importance in the life of the
group. Participants in a group laboratory are often surprised

at the changes in ability to listen from the earlier meetings to
the later ones, after shortcomings in listening are identified.
This difficulty can readily be recognized by playing back tape-
recorded sessions which enable the members to go over what
was actually said, and to compare this to what they thought they
heard. Taking questionnaire appraisals anonymously from time
to time may help the group to estimate its progress and to identify discrepancies in communication.

Thelen has developed a device which dramatizes the differences
between open versus private reception to a communication. A
panel of red and green lights is set up so that each member has
switch controls at his own chair. He can accept or agree with
a communication by switching on a green light, or he can show
disagreement by pressing the button for a red light. Since the
signals may be operated inconspicuously, the identity of the
group member is protected. Now it is possible to compare
one's own ideas about what is said with the opinion of other persons, and to check whether or not the group as a whole is re-
sponding as one thought they would. This instrument is particularly useful for experimental work in small group communication. As mentioned above under role, some specialization usually takes place in role differentiation with some members acting as information givers, others as questioners, etc. Problem
solving and decision making may be seen as aspects of the resolution of communication conflicts. Formal communication, such
as in teaching or in industry, may be distorted or blocked, depending upon the needs and problems of the informal communication system. Some leaders or experts are less productive than
others, not because they are inferior in technical skill, but because they may create barriers to communication without being
aware of these barriers in their relationships with others.

Listening

Listening may be a simple thing, as when we hear someone
tell us directions to the post office. It is another matter in a
group where people have come together to work on significant
issues. Listening is a skill which is imbedded in one's attitude
toward the immediate group and bears significantly on the personal qualities of the individual. Listening takes time and a
special effort in attending to the speaker and to the communication process. Some pertinent questions for effective listening
are noted. Do I understand literally what the other person is
saying? To whom is the comment addressed? What is the
speaker's frame of reference? What are the feelings which he
wishes to convey? Do I understand what he wants to get across?

Do I understand the feelings and ideas he is actually expressing, whether or not he is aware of these? Can I respond to what the speaker is intending to express? Am I aware of the context in which the comment is made? Am I aware of particular difficulties in my comprehension of certain individuals, or of communication under certain conditions?

These questions are presented as suggestions of the kinds of processes to which listening is related. It is surprising to see how infrequently people will check with each other to see if they understand each other correctly. Preoccupation with one's own thoughts and one's own anxieties, as well as unawareness of important group processes, may interfere with listening. As individuals learn to work together, they discover many ways of checking with each other (feedback), so that distortions are minimized. In a way, a maturing group becomes a self-correcting entity. Here too, progress can be noted by comparing early and late recordings of a group's interactions. Sometimes highly charged issues may reduce the self-correcting quality of group communication. In such instances, it may prove helpful to assign one person (or, if necessary, to bring one in from outside) who is skilled as an observer. The observer may then help the group in reestablishing its self-correcting communication process.

Humor, Rumor, and the Unknown in Group Life

In this outline, humor and rumor are treated as special manifestations of the communication process. Social psychologists have studied rumor formation and the spread of rumor, particularly during wartime or periods of crisis. Rumors tend to develop when there is a strong need to know what is going on but, for various reasons, information and communication are limited. Wartime censorship and lapses in communication present fertile soil for the growth of rumors. Rumors reflect the anxiety and the hopes of individuals as they attempt to piece together what is unknown from the little that is known. Tolerance for ambiguity and for unknowns is a personality characteristic as well as a function of group behavior. Since we can never know everything or even a major part of the feelings and thoughts of interacting group members, and since most groups are continually undergoing change as they work on new problems, the group situation continually generates rumors. Rumors may be viewed as a way of structuring the group. Unexpressed feelings in general and silent members in particular tend to stimulate rumors. Rumors also flourish around regions of high potential, i.e., around persons or sub-groups exerting strong influence.

NB

Humor, too, may be related to group tension and the unknown. Group relevant feelings, when brought into the open suddenly and in a manner which is not too threatening, may precipitate a discharge of feeling with an accompanying sense of relief. Groups often generate themes or processes of particular importance to the life of the group, and it is around these themes that indigenous humor may arise. Jokes may be made, for instance, about taking the initiative or about the degree of structure, and these humorous events may then become a part of the group culture. Because humor touches on vital matters, albeit in a special and limited way, it facilitates communication and decision making. Humor may, of course, serve as a means of expressing hostility in the group and may be exercised at the expense of some person or sub groups. Or humor may be a means of temporary flight from the situation at hand. There is probably no limit of the kinds of processes to which humor may be related. Both rumor and humor may take place outside of the physical setting of the group--but this, nevertheless, has some influence on the face-to-face group meeting itself.

Leadership and Power

One of the most important questions of group life concerns the meaning of leadership. The special influence exerted by one individual over others has fascinated and puzzled men throughout recorded history. In the small face-to-face group, leadership has been studied in natural and in experimental settings, and is invariably related to issues such as the power to reward and punish, the physical and organizational setting, the kind of problems or work confronting the group, the knowledge and special skills of members, and personality variables in the leader and in the followers. Leadership has been explored with reference to the cultural and historical conditions in which the total situation is imbedded, communication or the means by which influence is expressed, overt and covert aspects of leader-follower behavior, and the psychogenesis of leadership within the family (20). Other studies focus on special problems in hierarchical organizations (45), leaderless groups, distributed leadership, consensus and morale, autocratic, democratic, and laissez-faire leadership, and training for leadership.

In a laboratory on group dynamics, where heterogeneous groups begin to function in an unstructured setting, problems of leadership invariably arise. It remains a significant issue throughout the life of the group, but particularly in the opening phases when the nominal leader clearly indicates that he will not assume the traditional leader role. Group members may experience considerable frustration, since their reasonable expectations are not met. However, they soon find that they can function when thrown on their own resources, and in addition are able to experience and to observe leadership phenomena emerge. Soon the situation, with respect to power and leadership, becomes sufficiently stabilized so that members find they can work quite adequately, and at the same time increase their understanding of leadership behavior. By calling attention to the leadership processes at appropriate times, group members are assisted in their understanding of these behaviors and ideas, while they are actually involved in the decision making activities. As Lewin points out, "Recent experiments have shown that the training of leaders is to a high degree dependent upon the sensitizing of their social perception. The good leader is able and ready to perceive more subtle changes in social atmosphere and is more correct in observing social meaning." (32)

Leadership--A Summary

a. The search for special characteristics in the personality of the leader has failed to yield convincing results. This applies as much to intelligence as it does to the so-called charismatic or magical quality of the leader.
b. Situational and organizational factors, such as the assignment of authority, the power to reward and to punish, cannot be overlooked in ascertaining the meaning and locus of leadership.
c. An important variable appears to be the ability to sense, to be aware of what is going on in oneself as well as what is happening in the group or organization.
d. The skill and competence to make a contribution to the task of the group and to the emotional processes appear to be significant qualities. These two kinds of skill may be distributed among different individuals in the group.
e. Qualities in the followers may influence the choice of leadership. The more authoritarian members may demand strong direction by one person, while the more equalitarian members are apt to value leaders who are responsive to individual and group feelings. (50)   *NB*
f. The leader's role may even include serving as the scapegoat of the group.
g. There is growing interest in studying the distribution of leadership functions among the members of the group.
h. One way of identifying leadership, consistent with field theory, is the idea that a member is a leader "whose pertinent frame of reference another person or group attempts to assume." (43)

i. Authoritarian and equalitarian leadership are seen as dimen-
    sions on a continuum by some writers (51). They suggest
    that it is possible to choose a leadership pattern by assess-
    ing accurately what the organizational situation requires,
    and under what direction and freedom the individuals can
    best work.

j. In the pioneer study on leadership in different experimental
    group atmospheres, Lewin, Lippitt and White (35) found
    that:

    1. Autocratic and laissez-faire groups were not as orig-
        inal in their work as democratic groups were. Nor was
        autocracy more efficient than democracy.
    2. There was more dependence and less individuality in
        autocratic groups.
    3. Under the democratic leader, there was more friend-
        liness and group-mindedness.
    4. Under autocratic leaders, there was more overt and
        covert hostility and aggression, including aggression
        against scapegoats.
    5. Although this study was carried out in a midwestern
        American community with ten-year-old boys, and the
        atmospheres were simulated autocracy, democracy,
        and laissez-faire, the results are sufficiently consis-
        tent with other knowledge of groups to encourage fur-
        ther speculation and experimentation.

Corrosive Effect of Authority on Human Relations

Although authority may be seen as an essential aspect of leadership and of social organization, its abuse can seriously disturb
interpersonal relations. A few sample behaviors showing cor-
rosion by authority are listed in abbreviated summary. These
symptoms are, of course, not exclusive to authority relations.

a. Setting up barriers--Person with authority begins to wall
    himself off from others more than is necessary; secretaries,
    special offices, red tape, etc.
b. Using people as tools--Relates to others as if they were in-
    struments to be used in carrying out his will; impersonal,
    dehumanizing.
c. No need to check self--Acts arbitrarily; sees no need for
    checking, because this authority feels he can do no wrong.
    The validity of his behavior is, for him, self-evident.
d. Exclusive, sticks to his own level--Relates to others in
    terms of position in hierarchy; glorifies elite, condescend-
    ing to subordinates.

Consider check sheet utilizing these qualities to determine leadership problems

e. Special language--Uses words, abbreviations, labels in special ways; federalese, or organizational slang; circumlocutions, talks around a point.

f. Eliminates opposition--Serious disagreements are not tolerated; demolishes or subjugates dissenter; no long-range working out of differences.

g. Pseudo-humility--Patronizing and sweet at one time, indifferent at other times.

h. Rules and conformity--Insists on ever growing body of rules and regulations; emphasizes conventional ways and conformity; tends to avoid the risks of change.

i. Dichotomizes--Things are right or wrong, yes or no, good or bad; little if any grays; intolerant of ambiguity.

j. No real relationships with subordinates--Selects men who will agree with him even when they don't agree; prefers adulation; seeks out sycophants.

k. When anxious, gets tough--Hard work; cracks down; use of power a convenient way to deny anxieties; buries self in work, yet not genuinely productive.

l. Anti-intraceptive--Denies softer part of self, i.e., feelings in general and things like tenderness, passive needs; psychological processes like defenses, conflict with self are denied. .

Habeas Emotum *

One step marking man's advance out of the Dark Ages, was the evolution of the writ of habeas corpus, around the twelfth century. In its earliest form it enabled a person to avoid trial by battle and to obtain trial by jury. Later, habeas corpus was firmly established in English law to end all forms of illegal custody. Meaning literally, "you should have the body. . .," habeas corpus are the opening words of the legal writ which had as its object the bringing of a party before a court or a judge. In the United States we inherited the idea of habeas corpus embedded in common law, and it became established in the federal constitution and in the laws of most of the states.

But that writ applies to a man's physical freedom and the question raised here is, do we need to assert the principle of psychological freedom in a writ of habeas emotum? Today, the courts deal with problems of civil, economic, political, and physical rights, and the realm of emotions is left as a private matter--as it should be. But man seems to long for some sense of justice in the exercise of his psychological freedom, particularly now that major institutions involving family and community traditions are changing so rapidly.

---

* Luft, J. "Habeas Emotum" in NTL Human Relations Training News, Spring, 1963.

Where can he get a fair hearing, to say nothing of an unhurried
reaction to this blend of thoughts and feelings which is so close
to his own selfness? Is it not true that all human relations im-
plicitly rely upon some code of justice? It is a way, after all,
of showing we do care, and this accountability is important for
feelings of belonging with others and for being one's self.

In a recent talk, the author suggested that a training group is,
at times, a trial, metaphorically speaking. It is a trial in which
each member, including the staff person, serves as prosecutor,
defendant, witness, judge, and jury. Not all at once, but eventually, each member performs every role. Behavioral incidents
are freely provided, charges are made, indictments are offered,
counter charges are developed, evidence is ascertained, wit-
nesses testify, judgments are passed and then rescinded as more
data is gathered and rules are generated, implicit laws are
agreed upon, a form of justice is acknowledged.

The trainer is first seen as judge, then jury, and then as an
expert witness. Later he is seen as a special member of the
group who is himself judged by common law.

Interpersonal and intrapersonal conflicts generate the most
significant charges and countercharges. The members divide
and take sides, sometimes overtly, often covertly.

What makes judgment so significant is that members are being
judged by scales made, at least in part, of their own handicraft.

Everyone has erred and failed before. Now, one has a second
chance. Although each falls short of his own standard and is so
judged, everyone is acquitted.

The most frequent crimes are emotional misdemeanors against
others. The most serious malfeasance is a violation against oneself. The victim in the latter instance usually sets up the most
stringent standards for evidence and for justice. The prosecu-
tion and the defense happen to reside in the same person.

It is a paradox that this kind of trial and judging takes place
only after a non-judgmental atmosphere has been established--
which means only that the more superficial customs of the common culture are swept aside or taken for granted. There is a
search for psychological order, and a kind of universal consti-
tutional law is finally recognized: a fundamental law of man and
his feelings. The mark of a group is its concern for human emo-
tion. The right to one's own feelings and the right to express
them is the keystone. Awareness of the feelings of others has
high premium. The exercise of these rights, so based, creates
a profound sense of freedom. And the individual finds himself
learning and changing as his implicit and explicit expressions
are noted, pondered upon and reacted to. Little wonder then

that strangers participating in this process, quickly become significant persons.

Even simple, everyday contacts between people are highly complex and often yield a residue of misunderstandings and emotional debris. By common, unverbalized agreement, we ignore many of these minor incongruencies. From experience we know that extraneous problems carry over to unrelated situations; e.g., Mr. A. is greeted in a cool or gruff manner by his colleague; Mr. A. is puzzled, but ascribes the coolness to something that may have happened at home or perhaps on the way to the office. But there is always the prospect that these simple incongruencies are significant and pertinent to the persons in interaction. Where and when can one ever become enlightened about them? Even with people we know well--or perhaps particularly with people we know well--there are always large areas of inconsistencies or unknowns in our interactions with them. And these misunderstandings yield a quota of miscarriages of justice.

If we can get away from the association of judging and justice with law and the courts, but think of their pertinence to everyday life, we can immediately note innumerable ways in which judging and justice are called for and invoked.

Certain kinds of children's play call for more judging and justice than others; e.g., sandlot baseball as against exploring an ant hill or playing house. Children seem to have a keen sense of what is just and unjust. Without going too far off the point, a man on a job invariably searches for and expects a fair evaluation as well as recognition for everything he does. Obviously, he is not going to be judged or evaluated on every single act-- this is neither feasible nor desired--yet deep within him is a longing for this fair acknowledgment.

What is, however, more germane to habeas emotum is that feelings, unlike work, are not planned or expressed with deliberation. By their nature they are spontaneous and often occur without warning. Yet, does not each individual long for an acceptance of these feelings, and particularly the negative or difficult ones, on fair and just grounds? And this means an opportunity for an unhurried hearing and an examination of contingencies as necessary.

In everyday life, as noted, there is usually neither the time nor the inclination, and often not the ability, to accord the expression of feeling a full and fair acknowledgment. Thus, we, and especially men, hide, disguise or control our natural tendencies to express ourselves as an integral whole being, feelings and all.

The way we temper and control feelings depends upon the reality and the fairness accorded by others to their expression.
Watch how a child seethes with indignation when he is constrain-
ed for reasons he neither understands cognitively nor grasps
intuitively.

Perhaps the longing for fairness or justice is an archetype* in
the sense that "it derives from the experience of the human race
and is present in the unconscious of the individual." It is per-
fect in no one and has of course many variations in different
cultures. But basically this sense of justice seems to exist in
all humans--in one form or another. Where this sense is seriously warped or stunted, it is seen as a major pathological
symptom for the individual as well as for his society.

Perhaps the decay of a society may be said to coincide with the
disregard for the emotional rights of others. Although it is recognized that psychological injustice can be found throughout
history, and very likely in most cultures, there is little doubt
that where it is widespread, society is in serious trouble. In
plays, novels, and poetry we often find the clearest distillation
of the meaning of emotional violation. Since many people continue to experience and to think of feelings anachronistically--
i.e., somewhat closer to the Dark Ages-- it is not surprising
to find fairly widespread emotional barbarism.

Emotional interchange need not be reduced to bland, mild re-
strained affairs. Authentic feelings are invariably rugged. But
there is a time for the kind of informal hearing and quest for
fair play wherever people interact emotionally. After all, life
is for people, people with feelings.

In this syllabus, discussion is limited as much as possible to
the special kind of trial phenomenon that transpires in a basic
laboratory group. It is obviously not the only significant thing
that happens in a training group. Invoking the metaphorical writ
of habeas emotum, means that a group lays aside its other activities for a while and gives precedence to the claimant who
demands a fair and open hearing.

Habeas emotum implies the right of the individual to have his
own feelings; it also means he has a right to express these feelings freely unless it can be shown that by so doing, he limits the
emotional freedom of others. Such conflicts are inevitable and
deserve a fair hearing commensurate with the significance of
these feelings for the individuals concerned. The broadest lati-
tude is accorded the litigants. In the pursuit of psychological
justice, new interactions precipitate additional data and evidence,

---

*The Unabridged Webster Dictionary definition of Jung's use of the term.

and the processes of gathering and weighing impressions and
observations are of prime importance. The trial calls for both
deep involvement and for objective observation, a most difficult
combination. The quality of consensus varies with the calibre
of the persons in the group, but more crucially by the nature of
the processes employed.

Reprinted by permission of United Features Syndicate and The San Francisco Chronicle.

One of the most important studies to call attention to the significance of informal groups in a large organizational setting
was the pioneering work of Mayo (39) and his associates. Beginning in 1927, Mayo tried to find relationships between physical conditions of work and the productivity of employees at a
large electrical manufacturing plant. He set up a control group
and an experimental group and proceeded to vary systemati-
cally the physical variables of light, heat, and humidity. Production rose as these conditions improved, but when he restored
the original conditions, he was surprised to find that worker
output remained at a high level. Only then did they probe the
attitudes of this group of workers. They found morale to be
quite high, partly because they were relieved of the usual supervision and partly because the workers enjoyed being singled
out for special attention by the experimenters. This change in
attitude among the workers seemed to be more important than
changes in physical working conditions. The results called
attention to the significance of small group processes which
exist informally outside the formal structure and organization
of the factory.
Another of the Mayo findings came from the depth interviews
of large numbers of workers. They learned that in spite of a
seemingly fine set of personnel policies, a very large number
of employees had all kinds of grievances and complaints. It
appeared that a sub-world of important attitudes and feelings
existed which were unknown to the supervisors and executives.
Furthermore, levels and standards of production were determined by these informal groups more than by management.
Workers sought acceptance and approval by their informal
groups rather than risk social rejection and ostracism. At
times, the pressures to conform to the group's standards, to
win the group's acceptance, was more important than financial
rewards.
Industrial managers began to discover anew that the worker
was human, and that his feelings and attitudes could not be taken
for granted. The industrial employee was no longer a special
kind of machine, he was not a slave nor a serf, but an individual
whose social and psychological needs reflected the political and
philosophical values of the society in which he lived. Industry
turned to sociologists and psychologists to learn more about
these informal groups, how their attitudes were formed and

36

how decisions were made (27). While some managers merely sought new ways of manipulating and controlling employees with knowledge gained from the social scientists, in general, they sought a better understanding of their industrial organizations. Workers, too, through their trade unions, began calling in inter-disciplinary experts to help them understand their problems affecting union management and the processes of collective bargaining.

Various universities throughout the country have tried to meet these needs by turning more attention to human relations research in industry. The Harvard Business Review, for example, is prominent in publishing articles and studies in this field. The Society for the Advancement of Management cooperates in various ways with social scientists, including the organization of workshops and seminars to learn more about the art and science of working with others.

When someone is honestly 55% right, that's very good and there's no use wrangling. And if someone is 60% right, it's wonderful, it's great luck and let him thank God. But what's to be said about 75% right? Wise people say this is suspicious. Well, and what about 100% right? Whoever says he's 100% right is a fanatic, a thug, and the worst kind of rascal.   An Old Galician

(Reprinted in Contemporary Psych., Febr. 1960.)

Ever since Freud's Psychopathology of Everyday Life (21).
a new light has been thrown on the garden variety of human
idiosyncracies. Illustrations such as the following one are com-
monplace and nearly every one can add his own supply. At the
beginning of a meeting of a conservative women's club recently,
a prominent radical was introduced by the chairlady with the
following slip of the tongue: ". . . It gives me great pleasure to
prevent . . . I mean present, the distinguished speaker . . . ."
What Freud contributed was a rich new source of ideas, of hypotheses, to the explanation of behavior.

Errors, slips of the tongue, lapses in memory, and many other
kinds of foibles could be interpreted in a more meaningful way
consistent with the unconscious, underlying purposive behavior
of the individual. There is a hazard here, of course, since not
everyone is a Freud in his skill and sensitivity in making inter-
pretations. If these ideas are seen as hypotheses which could
be checked and tested against other observations and evidence,
then we can recognize that a genuine contribution has been made
to the understanding of behavior.

Clinicians in psychology and in psychiatry deal constantly with
the major and minor deviations of human activity. Increasingly,
it has become clear that the differences which exist between the
normal and the abnormal are differences in degree rather than
in kind.

The vast and growing experience in studying and treating the
disturbed, the anxious, and the pathological has improved our
understanding of the sound and healthy population. This does
not mean that every human act can or should be viewed from a
clinical orientation. It means rather we are becoming increasingly free of the tendency to see behavior as right or wrong,
sick or well, good or bad, but simply human behavior as it actually is.

The clinician's understanding of behavior is moving further
away from the categories and types which preoccupied him until
fairly recently. The expert tries to comprehend the full complexities or what is called the "psychodynamics of behavior,"
rather than attempting to pin a label, a diagnostic category, on
his patient.

The major divisions of work of the clinical psychologist con-
sist of diagnosis, therapy, and research. Like the specialists
in group dynamics, he is painfully aware of the tremendous gaps
in his knowledge and of the tentativeness of much of his present

understanding, and for this reason places highest emphasis upon the need for further investigation, study, and research. Nevertheless, it is necessary to try to put together the best ideas and the best comprehension of the present, even though tomorrow's findings may invalidate some of them.

The work of the people in group dynamics can be divided in roughly the same way as that of the clinician's. Diagnosis here means observation (usually as participant-observer), measurement (attitude scales, sociometric devices), and assessment of the behavior in the group; it means trying to understand, with whatever tools and techniques are available, the interactions of group members. The end product of diagnosis of group behavior is precisely comparable to that of the modern clinician--a better understanding of the dynamics of group life. Not a label, not a number, not a type, but working jointly with members toward an accurate description of what is observed, together with a carefully formulated series of hypotheses about what the behavior signifies.

For the clinician, the second major division of work is therapy; for the group dynamics specialist it means helping the members of the group to find out more clearly what they want to do, and the methods by which they might move toward their own goals. This is particularly true of laboratory groups. Very often the goal is to increase effectiveness if it is primarily a work or task group, while at the same time increasing the satisfactions of the individual member. Just as the modern clinician knows that his job is not to make the plans or decisions but to aid the patient in working through his ownproblems, so, too, the student of group dynamics recognizes that the group members themselves can best establish goals, work through problems, and make their own decisions.

Interrelationship Between Diagnosis and Treatment

Diagnosis and psychotherapy are actually inseparable processes for the clinician. As the therapist learns more about the problems and the history of the patient, the patient is already at work trying to express what he feels and what he makes of his problems. By carefully determined interventions, by clarification, by reflection and interpretation, the therapist encourages greater understanding. Every new insight by the patient, every change in feeling, is accompanied by new thoughts, new memories. These therapeutic changes in the patient, then, bring out new thoughts and feelings for the therapist who can now improve his understanding of the psychodynamics of his particular patient.

In applied group dynamics, too, we find that diagnosing the
problem and doing something about the problem are inseparable. The more the group finds out about its own processes.
the more information and feelings can be brought out. The con-
sultant to the group can then continue to enrich his picture of
the dynamics of this group and to facilitate greater comprehension of group processes. As new insights and information grow,
the work of the group toward resolving its own problems moves
ahead, bringing with this change additional ideas and feelings in
a continuous spiral of progress.

The field of clinical psychology, like the field of group dynamics, is both a theoretical science and an applied art. Although
notable progress has been made, both fields are struggling with
large and serious problems arising out of the dilemma of being
both pure and applied. For instance, clear scientific evidence
for the value of psychotherapy has not yet been established, even
though there are many face validity indicators of its effectiveness. Nevertheless, the clinician must continue to work in therapy for many reasons, including the need to do something based
on the best knowledge available. The clinician is rewarded, as
Freud found out, by opportunities for the study of psychological
disorder and for improving the methods of psychotherapy. But
there are other great problems--the problem of training new
and better psychotherapists, the problem of ethics of the prac-
titioner, the thorny problem of personal values, the responsibility for guarding confidential information while at the same
time needing more and more to make public the results so that
scientific check is possible. In group dynamics, the very same
issues are being discussed and fought over; the same hazards
and opportunities exist.

Contributions of Freud and Rogers

Freud's theories have had such enormous impact on the social
sciences that it would be beyond the scope of this paper to
attempt a summary. However, the psychoanalytic point of view
has been applied fruitfully to the study of face-to-face groups
and will be briefly touched on here. Psychoanalysts tend to
make fewer distinctions between the activity of psychotherapy
groups and other kinds of collective behavior. The basic model
is, of course, the family. All groups are seen as modifications
of family life. Leaders are viewed from the point of view of the
psychodynamics of parent-child relationships. Unconscious
strivings of group members are given greatest importance.
Love and hate, pain and pleasure, the strictures of super-ego
versus demands of primitive impulse, are the basic motivations

and sources of conflict. The development and capabilities of
the ego constitute the coping mechanism of the group members.
Psychological defenses, their growth and dissolution comprise
important processes in the group. Transference and counter-
transference among group members account for many of the
"irrationalities" and conflicts. Although cultural pressures
and external work requirements are acknowledged as significant
forces in group processes, the emotional factors in intrapersonal and interpersonal dynamics are the most important deter-
minants.

Unstructured groups are seen as arousing the latent unresolved,
unconscious conflicts in the group members. Progress consists
in working through these conflicts in a permissive atmosphere,
so that more energy and ability can be applied to the realities
of the group situation.

Rogers (44) has made major contributions to clinical psychology and to the study and treatment of personality disorders.
After acknowledging his indebtedness to the germinal work of
Freud, he departs from the psychoanalytic tradition and takes
strong issue with orthodox Freudians, particularly on the question of unconscious motivation, transference, and the directive
activities of the therapist.

Rogers holds that the individual is basically guided by inner
needs for growth, health, and self-actualization. Personality
problems develop when individual freedom is threatened or in-
terfered with. These negative pressures distort the individual's
perception of self and of others, and result in loss of self-esteem
and feelings of security. To the extent that the individual loses
trust in his own feelings and perceptions, he retards his potential for growth and self-actualization. In addition, he feels alien-
ated with himself and may develop various physical and psychological symptoms of anxiety. The problem of the therapist is
to encourage communication between client and therapist, so
that the client may be able to rediscover (insight) those thoughts
and feelings which are really his own. The therapeutic process
calls for the closest kind of listening by the therapist so as to
see things as the client sees them, and to identify feelings
which the client is actually trying to express. The therapist
does not guide or direct the client's thoughts, feelings, or plans.
As the client feels more secure in the permissive situation, he
can bring out more of his real feelings, although initially he
finds himself permeated with critical feelings toward himself
and his own worth. As these are accepted, without valuation or
interpretation by the therapist, the client is encouraged to bring
out more painful or hidden feelings, until he begins to arrive at

a more balanced picture of himself. Emphasis throughout is on respect for the independence of the client; Rogers and his associates have found that the client does not experience the disabling dependency which accompanies the more directive kinds of therapy.

In a group situation, whether it be an administration work group, a seminar, or a therapy group, the basic phenomenological principles are essentially the same for Rogers. The emphasis is on self-directiveness of the group, on permissiveness so that threat is reduced and communication freed, on sensitivity to feelings and the importance of listening to what is actually being expressed, rather than dwelling on the interpretation of behavior. These principles, greatly condensed here, are seen as the prime matters of group life, and if faithfully carried through will enable a group to develop its own goals more adequately and move toward their achievement.

Group Dynamics and Group Psychotherapy

If we restrict ourselves to the laboratory method for studying group dynamics, we might profitably consider in what ways group dynamics seminars differ from group psychotherapy. It has already been mentioned that the group dynamics laboratories encourage settings which are similar in some ways to the settings for group psychotherapy. The group is usually small enough so that all members can converse easily with all other members; this usually means anywhere from about five to fifteen persons. The general structure of the groups is also similar, in that minimal orientation is given and a large degree of ambiguity exists. Also the designated leader in group process laboratories takes a relatively passive role, as does the group therapist.

However, important differences do exist. First, the agreement (or informal contract) between patient and therapist is different from the agreement between the student of group dynamics and the laboratory instructor. The patient asks for alleviation of psychological symptoms of personal distress; the student asks for an opportunity to learn an academic and applied discipline. The patient may be suffering from neurotic or psychotic condition; the student is essentially a normal, healthy individual who wants to improve his knowledge and skill in working with others.

Second, in the group dynamics laboratory, ideas and feelings are explored as they have a bearing on the processes of the group. Heightened awareness of group processes is of crucial importance in group dynamics, and learning about one's own feelings and behavior, one's impact on others and the pattern of one's relationships in the group are involved in this growing awareness. It is relevant to consider attitudes of members in the group about the group; it is not relevant to trace the origins and early family sources of these attitudes. In group therapy, feelings of group members toward each other are explored as well as early family origins. In group therapy, dreams and other projective associations may be openly dealt with. In group dynamics there is more strict adherence to the "here and now." Deep unconscious conflicts are not analyzed or examined in the group dynamics laboratory.

Third, group dynamics laboratories are of relatively short duration; a few days or weeks, or possibly a semester. Group therapy may go on for years, and may be supplemented by individual psychotherapy.

Fourth, group dynamics laboratories aim primarily toward cognitive change, learning of ideas, concepts, and theories, although in a more limited sense they would be interested in behavioral or attitudinal change as well.

Alexander and French (2), in their discussion of brief psychoanalytic psychotherapy, insist that a "corrective emotional experience" is essential for personality change and growth. They state that a corrective emotional experience may occur not only in psychotherapy, but also in everyday life, as illustrated by the hero in Victor Hugo's Les Miserables. When Jean Valjean steals the silver candlesticks of the bishop who befriended him, and is later caught by the police, the bishop refuses to see this as theft but rather as a gift to a man who needed the silver more than he did. Jean Valjean is stunned by this unexpected reaction and he is forced into a re-evaluation of his own worth. For him, it is the beginning of great changes in his outlook and behavior.

A corrective emotional experience may occur in formal schooling, although it is certainly not a common event. It may occur in the family, in business, or in contact with the arts. It may also occur in a group dynamics laboratory where conditions are favorable for gaining new glimpses of one's relationships with others.

Group therapy may result in the acquisition of new knowledge, but this is not a primary goal. The group dynamics student wants to learn principles and generalizations so that he may better understand all kinds of groups and particularly his work group or social group back home. Consequently, the group laboratories schedule lectures, theory sessions, and content seminars to broaden the base of learning. In addition, books, journals, and articles are made available in a library or reading room which is an integral part of the laboratory.

Over a half-century ago, William James (24) told teachers
that the science of psychology had little to offer which would
aid them in their daily work.

"I say moreover that you make a great, a very great mistake,
if you think that psychology, being the science of the mind's
laws, is something from which you can deduce definite pro-
grammes and schemes and methods of instruction for immediate schoolroom use. Psychology is a science, and teaching is
an art; and sciences never generate arts directly out of themselves. An intermediary inventive mind must make the application, by using its originality."

The volume of research and publications has increased tre-
mendously since then, but the teacher has not been overwhelmed
with knowledge he can use. He stands pretty much as he did
then--he stands on his own. The comments offered here are
not designed to show the teacher how to teach; rather they are
intended to call to the teacher's attention certain group relevant
characteristics of his work. By emphasizing group processes
in teaching and learning, the teacher may find it useful to re-
consider some basic problems with which he is confronted daily.

Unfortunately, many people think of group dynamics as a collection of techniques and methods. As mentioned earlier, group
dynamics is the study of behavior in groups. One may study
riot mobs, or church services, or a team of scientists, or a
teacher conducting a class. Group dynamics does not tell us
what a group should or should not do. It does not advocate doing
things in groups, nor does it mean sweetness and light in group
behavior.

A colleague once told this writer that he was opposed to group
dynamics because he personally disliked committee work. He
might just as well have said he opposed biology because he
hated raw green vegetables.

Here are some questions which a teacher may ask because
they have a bearing on his work and on group processes:

a. How can I get my pupils to work harder and to learn more?
   Is group motivation part of my job?
b. What about discipline? Are disciplinary actions related to
   group behavior?
c. How can I communicate more effectively with my class?
d. To what extent should my pupils determine what is to be
   studied and how they are to be evaluated?
e. To what extent do I follow a predetermined plan for my
   class? To what extent do I permit changes in my over-all
   plan and changes in my daily plan?

44

f. Is classroom morale any of my business? Or does it take care of itself so long as I keep to my teaching?
g. What relation is there between how I get along with my school superiors and my classroom work? The same question can be raised in connection with my colleagues.
h. Should the teacher have a hand in setting school policy? Or is this just not the teacher's job?
i. What about curriculum? Is it the teacher's concern and, if so, how does one go about influencing curriculum change?
j. Does it help to think of oneself as a leader in the classroom? What kind of leader should a teacher be? How do I find out what kind of a leader I am?
k. What about parents? How do I learn to work more effectively with them?
l. What about my own improvement in my field of specialization? Are my own studies and intellectual growth a personal matter, or is it also a function of group processes in the school?
m. Should the teacher carry special responsibilities outside of school? Who decides about the role of the teacher in the community?
n. Is it possible to improve my skill in working with groups without becoming a manipulator of people? What about ethics in group dynamics?

Some of these are age-old questions which are still not answerable. Others are beyond the scope of this syllabus. But all have some relation to the teacher and the group, and the discussion which follows attempts to highlight this relationship.

The teacher is both a participant with his class and an observer. He needs to explain, give information, ask questions, challenge, listen, think, recognize individual and group differences, stimulate, give support and inspire, among other things. And he hopes to follow some over-all plan so that his work with his pupils ties in with what went before and with what will follow.

Then, too, he must recognize the needs and demands of his school superiors, his boss, and of his colleagues, to say nothing of parents and their questions, problems, and demands. But perhaps most important is the teacher's knowledge and awareness of himself, his strengths and weaknesses, his own needs and his own blind spots.

This adds up to a tremendous order. And from all quarters we find people eager to criticize the teacher, to point out his shortcomings. But what can be offered to help him? More specifically, why add to his burden by calling attention to group dynamics? If, as James pointed out, teaching is an art, what should the teacher know about groups in order to improve his skill?

A group may be thought of as a developing system with its own structure, organization, and norms. Classes may look alike from a distance, or on paper--but actually each class is as unique as a fingerprint. Each class develops its own internal procedures and pattern of interactions, and its own limits. It is as if imaginary lines were guiding and controlling behavior within the group. In spite of day by day variation, there is a certain constancy in each class which emerges from its individual history.

The teacher may be able to recognize qualities, such as interdependency, which characterize the way the pupils work. And the teacher might speculate about what it is that he does to enable the group to become more independent and more interdedependent. How to encourage individuality in his pupils, while at the same time teaching them the value of consideration for others, is another way of looking at the goals of the group. Pupils cannot learn this by merely reading books or from listening to lectures. It comes from working with other people as a supplement to working alone. What he learns from infancy on in his own family is of course fundamental to what he is. Because each family is, in fact, another group with its particular qualities, the child carries over certain expectations into his classroom group.

The main point to be emphasized here is that group life, per se, is an important reality; that a growing body of scientific knowledge exists concerning principles of group processes; and, finally, that through particular kinds of experience it is possible for the teacher to become more effective in working with groups.

There could be considerable value for the teacher in learning more about his own behavior in groups. It is possible, of course, to learn this from experience. Or, the teacher may participate in group laboratories or workshops especially designed to help him become more aware of his characteristic interactions. Some reasons for laboratory learning about groups are noted:

a. To take the time to explore the factors influencing the teacher's own motivation in learning and in teaching. In a permissive group, it becomes possible to clarify deeper motives. In learning about his own tendencies to "dress up" his motives, the teacher might better appreciate the same problems in his pupils.

b. To recognize the development and power of group norms. By actually experiencing the development of a group norm and its power to guide or restrict the individual, a teacher can more intimately grasp the significance of these norms in pupil groups. Pressure toward conformity and the hostility toward those who violate group norms have an important bearing on classroom learning.

c. To learn about social and personal obstacles to learning. Groups can be cruel or gentle with a sensitive or a typical pupil. To learn something about these prevailing atmospheres, it is useful for the teacher to again live through these experiences, but this time in a group where such things can be identified, clarified, and understood.

d. To distinguish between surface appearance of groups and the covert life that may not be apparent, but still is highly important. In other words, a group may seem to be working very well, orderly, quiet, and going through the correct motions. Only, nothing really happens, nothing changes, nothing is learned. A sound group, a class where pupils are working and learning, may not always look very productive to an outsider.

e. To learn more about the value of self-determination in groups. As a class learns to guide itself, to take on more responsibility, the pupils learn more out of intrinsic motives (7). The pupil does more to learn and to acquire for himself, and he learns to work with others at the same time.

f. To become more aware of the variety of leadership functions. The teacher, as a special kind of leader, should understand more about the different kinds of leadership patterns, such as centralized or distributed functions, formal and informal leadership, the emergence of pupil leaders and of leadership in sub-groups, and the effect of these patterns on the teacher's work.

g. To recognize the teacher's power as a leader so that his use of rewards and punishments is in line with the learning goals. At the same time, the teacher needs to learn about the group's power to reward and to punish its own members, and its ability to influence the teacher.

h. To learn about the evolution of status and role within a classroom group. The basis for status may be school grades and intelligence, but it may also include social skills, physical prowess, ability to defy authority (37), and other emotional capacities which have little direct relation to the learning of academic subject matter itself.

We take for granted that a teacher is well informed, particularly in his field of specialization. His knowledge and his ability to acquire continually new knowledge are basic to his work.

But what is less well understood and less well appreciated are the more subtle skills required to work with a classful of twenty, thirty or forty young people.

Standing alone in the classroom, the teacher has little to guide him except what he knows, what he observes and understands, what he senses and feels. His superiors, his colleagues, parents, and the community are looking over his shoulder. He must be sensitive to what is going on while he works, somewhat as an artist, in moving toward his learning-teaching objectives. The rules and plans of the school can seem quite remote and abstract; here are the pupils reacting intensely with strong curiosity, or apathetically, at any given moment. The teacher needs to learn to trust his own senses, his own observations. He must recognize the realities of group life as well as the complexities of individual personality. If he is well aware of his own impact on others he can work to influence the class in a more desirable direction. If he is blind to his own motives and to his own behavior, he may work hard and yet defeat his own purposes.

In effect, this amounts to asking the teacher to "know thyself," that ancient appeal which is so widely known and even more widely ignored. For to learn more about oneself in relation to others is not only difficult and time consuming, it is apt to arouse unsuspected anxiety. Without this awareness, we often see rigid, authoritarian methods imposed on teachers and pupils. And on the other hand, mistakes of an equally flagrant sort occur when well intentioned but misinformed teachers loosen all controls and a misguided permissiveness in the classroom results. This can be recognized by an atmosphere of indifference diffused through the class; very little is learned, and pupils tend to become bored or merely mischievous.

Like the artist who steps back frequently to observe more clearly his emerging work, the teacher needs open and effective communication with his class so that he may perceive more clearly what is going on. He needs to stop, to observe, and to listen. If the atmosphere is sufficiently free, he will obtain an adequate picture of what is going on and of what needs to be done. If the teacher can accept some of the negative feelings in himself, he may be better able to accept pupils as they are. And he may be better able to tolerate and to deal with group hostility and classroom anxiety. For these feelings are bound to develop as pupils, with their diverse backgrounds and expectations, learn to work together.

If the teacher can be more aware and more open about his own abilities and limitations, he may help to generate more

trust in his pupils. He will have less need to hide behind his
official status. He, the teacher, may be more open to the new
ideas and new information from his pupils, and from others as
well. By dispensing with the spurious privileges of his status,
he may be freer to concentrate on the subject matter and on the
learning process. Pupils, sensing this more authentic atmosphere, may respond with greater curiosity and effort in their
work. The results may not be as neat and as uniform as some
critics would like, but it will further the achievements of the
individual and of the class as a whole. By accepting pupils' dependency needs and by encouraging participation and involvement, the class may grow in ability to govern itself and to work
more on its own. This implies that the teacher is willing to
work with each collection of pupils as a unique group. Going
through the motions of group participation and group decision
making, but subtly retaining all control, is simply manipulation.
If a teacher cannot or will not trust his pupils to have a real
voice in class work or class decisions, he could at least be
open and aboveboard about it.

On Groups and Methods

Thus far, nothing has been said about group methods and techniques. Frequently, teachers want to know specifically what
they might do under particular circumstances. The main point
to be made here is that learning "methods" of working with
groups can be rather futile or worse, if the method is not based
on understanding.

Parents similarly ask, "What do I do when. . ." type questions.
It is difficult to impress upon them that a specific situation may
be far more complicated than it seems--or it may actually be
different than what the parent perceives.

Teachers may want to know what to do when, for instance,
there seems to be an outbreak of restlessness or of apathy among
the pupils. It is simply not possible to indicate what should be
done without knowing what produced these widespread feelings
in the class. But the teachers can learn to find out. They might
inquire and observe and attend to what is happening. They might
express a willingness to become more aware of what is going
on--without judging too critically. There are many different
ways of reducing tension and of resolving conflicts, and a teacher
may learn to sense what method would be appropriate for him
under these circumstances. One teacher might be able to change
the group atmosphere by asking the class what is going on, what
it is they feel, so that all can face the ongoing reactions more
openly. Arithmetic or reading lessons may stop temporarily,

so that pupils can express themselves and thereby work on meeting or resolving emotional needs.

Another teacher might achieve equivalent results by suggesting pupils work in smaller groups so that they can work and talk more informally and more freely. Children frequently work out their own problems of interpersonal relations and may be encouraged to do so. Of course, the teacher may need to establish limits, but these should be broad and realistic.

Viewing the class as a working group may change the teacher's perception of the classroom itself. The chairs, the tables, and the floor space should serve the particular work needs. Sometimes the work will demand that pupils discuss and plan together. To see each other and be able to talk and work as a group may call for a circular or rectangular arrangement of chairs and tables. For smaller work groups, tables may be distributed around the room. Sometimes the work will suggest a chair arrangement without tables, etc. In short, once the teacher frees himself from a conventional teacher-centered approach to class work, he may think of many different teaching methods as well as different uses of physical facilities to aid the teaching-learning process.

Often, a teacher will respond intuitively to a change in the atmosphere of a group, and this is fine. However, when his intuition does not work, can the teacher find out why? How, in other words, can the teacher improve on his intuition?

Teachers learn a great deal by discussing their classroom experiences with others. Unfortunately, many teachers feel it is not wise nor discreet to talk over their work frankly, for fear of adverse reactions. Consequently, they impose a quiet censorship over their classroom problems and experience. Teachers need to be able to discuss these matters freely and frankly with persons who are skilled and sensitive to their problems.

It would be fine if every teacher could have access to non-judgmental experts who would listen and clarify and instruct. But since such a resource does not usually exist, the next best thing is to be able to discuss these matters with colleagues. And free discussions with colleagues and with superiors call for an atmosphere of mutual trust where a teacher can admit weaknesses, errors or anxieties without fear of negative appraisal. And it would be even more effective if the teachers could sit in on each other's classes occasionally and observe how others handle problems and how they apply methods. Then the observer and the teacher observed could get together to discuss what went on as each one saw it.

There is probably no limit to the number of ways in which

teachers can improve their teaching skill. It would be naive to underestimate the complexities of the problems involved in the large organizations which schools have become. What is emphasized here is the reality of group life, how group processes affect the teacher and the pupils, and some opening ideas about what might be done in order to become more aware of the learning teaching experience. Attention is called to the significance of classroom atmosphere and the underlying variables which influence group and individual motivation.

Motivation to learn may be seen as a function of the needs of the individual child and of the needs of the group. A pupil may have a need to understand the world around him and the world of ideas; that is, intellectual needs. He also has social or group needs, the need to belong, to be accepted by his peers, the need to be understood, the need to express himself, and the need for esteem and for status. He has emotional needs which also affect his learning; his need for affection, his need to be dependent, to be nurtured, to be assertive, to be alone, to be creative, to be secure, his need to take chances and to explore and to change and to grow--among many other basic needs. Although it is obviously impossible for either the school or for the teacher to meet all these needs, they nevertheless exist, and have some bearing on classroom behavior and learning.

A class as a group may have a need to participate with the teacher in setting goals and establishing structure, developing its norms for behavior, its channels and means of communication. A group may need to build or reduce tension, which is related to strength of motivation. A group may need to test the limits which govern its behavior, and to test before it trusts its teachers and its leaders. A class as a group may have needs to make its own mistakes, to learn by its own experience as well as by the experience of its teachers and the recorded experience of others in books.

Lewin, Rogers and others have emphasized that learning requires a change in perception. If punishment is heavily relied upon to motivate the pupil, then the learner's field may be restricted but it does not assure that he will acquire the new knowledge or new insight. If the pupil's efforts are met with friendly interest so that he finds it satisfying to consider small changes in his own perceptions, he may be making progress toward reexamining and restructuring the whole context under consideration. In short, the pupil will entertain new perceptions; i.e., he will learn. He will develop his own questions which will serve as a purpose for his newer inquiries. Intrinsic motives, learning because he wants to know, will replace extrinsic motives.

When a group of pupils develops norms such that new perceptions and new questions are part of the group's own purpose or
goals, then the learning process will have been greatly strength-
ened for the individual learner. As Lewin's work has shown, a
group attitude toward change can often be more powerful in
supporting new learning in its members than individual isolated
efforts.

The teacher's task is to develop an atmosphere conducive to
new group perceptions. Methods and techniques devised by the
teacher to encourage pupil's participation in the work of the
class will increase the learner's readiness for new ideas and
new attitudes. Since, in the final analysis, new knowledge must
be absorbed and integrated with what the pupil now perceives
and understands, he can do this better by participating with his
peers and with his teacher, so that his questions and directions
are integrated in the work of the class. The pupil will not only
feel himself to be part of the class instead of a passive observer,
he will also be contributing to its goals and procedures.

Though a common base of knowledge and ideas will be shared,
pupils will vary in their learning depending on their ability, on
their needs and on their experience. Each child will have a
shared frame of reference, a shared body of knowledge, as well
as a unique context and a unique learning achievement.

The teacher's awareness of the phenomenon of group cohesiveness will point up the value of meeting the pupil's need to be
accepted and to belong. At the same time, he will be alert to
the pressures on the pupil to conform to the prevailing code of
the group. If, in the development of group norms, minority
voices are not permitted, then the class will have lost its potential for new change and new ideas. And a rigid uniformity could
result. Very small incidents in the early life of the group can
serve to indicate whether it will be safe and acceptable to express original or deviate ideas. The teacher will be sensitive
to these events if he understands how groups develop, and how
group standards and group atmospheres are formed.

A Word About the School As a Whole

The school itself is, of course, a large organization. As a
group of people, there are, again, the interactions and struc-
tures which have an important bearing on the individual teacher
and on the individual pupil. Greater awareness of the group
processes in a school as a whole can help the individual teacher
to understand what is going on. He can relate the fluctuations
of morale of teachers and of pupils to the various group relevant
behaviors of persons and sub-groups in the total school setting.

By working toward the clarification of processes when necessary the teacher may be able to influence the school as a whole,
at least to the extent that it has implications for his work. Cyni-
cism in the teaching staff, for instance, may be seen more clearly in relation to some misapplication of power than to a defect
of one person's character. Awareness of group interaction in
a school may counteract the tendency to ascribe difficulties on
the job to personality weakness. Unfortunately, the search for
the "flaw in character" seems to be a fairly common practice
in schools, as it is in too many large organizations.

A teacher's effectiveness depends to a considerable extent on
his relationships with his fellow teachers and his relationship
with his superiors. Just as his pupils are able to spot petty de-
fensiveness and the playing of favorites in the classroom, so too
can the teachers quickly sense the misuse of authority by their
superiors. But the superiors are also dependent on the teachers.
A teacher's sensitivity to the needs of the formal authorities
may help his superiors to feel more accepted by his staff. A
teacher can help the head of the school become more aware of
the school's group processes. And it would help everyone to be
able to discuss these things in non-judgmental terms.

Although the specific content is different, the goals of the larger group in the school are similar to the classroom group:
greater independence and interdependence in the teaching staff,
distributed leadership functions (7) between the school head
and teachers wherever this is appropriate, the clarification of
the principal's role and responsibilities, the improvement of
communication between administrators and teaching staff, the
application of the principal's power in a fair and realistic manner, the encouragement of individuality and creativity among the
teachers within the broadly defined goals of the school. Relations
between the school and the community can be strongly influenced
by staff collaboration, so that the teachers are supported in their
efforts and protected against unnecessary interference with their
work. These are only some of the tasks and goals of group relations in a school setting.

Reprinted by permission of United Features Syndicate and The San Francisco Chronicle.

1. Asch, S. E. Social Psychology. New York: Prentice-Hall, 1952.

2. Alexander, Franz and French, M. T. Psychoanalytic Therapy. New York: Ronald Press, 1946.

3. Back, K. "Influence Through Social Communication," Journal of Abnormal and Social Psychology, 46, 1951, pages 9-23.

4. Bales, Robert F. Interaction Process Analysis. Cambridge, Mass.: Addison-Wesley Press, 1950.

5. Bavelas, A. "Some Problems of Organizational Change," Journal of Social Issues, IV, No. 3, 1948, pages 48-52.

6. Baritz, Loren. The Servants of Power, a history of the use of social science in American industry. Wesleyan University Press, 1960.

7. Benne, K. D. and Muntyan, B. Human Relations in Curriculum Change. New York: Dryden Press, 1951.

8. Benne, K. D. and Sheats, P. "Functional Roles of Group Members," Journal of Social Issues, IV, No. 2, 1948, pages 41-49.

9. Bion, W. R. "Experiences in Groups," Human Relations, I, 1948, pages 314-329; 487-496.

10. Bovard, E. W. Jr. "The Psychology of Classroom Interaction," Journal of Educational Research, 45, 1951, pages 215-224.

11. Cattell, R. B. "New Concepts of Measuring Leadership," Group Dynamics. D. Cartwright and A. Zander, eds. Evanston, Ill.: Row, Peterson, and Co., 1956.

12. Cartwright, D. "Emotional Dimensions of Group Life," International Symposium on Feelings and Emotions. M. L. Reymert, ed. New York: McGraw-Hill Book Co., Inc., 1950.

13. Cartwright, D. and Zander, A. (eds.) Group Dynamics, Research and Theory, 2nd ed. Evanston, Ill.: Row, Peterson and Co., 1960.

14. Coch, Lester and French, John R. P. Jr. "Overcoming Resistance to Change," Human Relations, I, 1948, pages 512-532.

15. Coffey, H. S. "Socio and Psyche Group Process, Integrative Concepts," Journal of Social Issues, VIII, 1952, pages 65-74.

16. Cooley, C. H. Human Nature and the Social Order. New York: Scribner. 1902.

17. Crutchfield, R. S. "Conformity and Character," American Psychologist, X, 1955, pages 191-198.

18. Crutchfield, R. S. "Social Psychology and Group Processes," Annual Review of Psychology, V, 1954, page 171.

19. Festinger, L.; Schacter, S.; and Back, K. Social Pressure in Informal Groups. New York: Harper, 1950.

20. Freud, Sigmund. Group Psychology and the Analysis of the Ego. London: Hogarth, 1922.

21. Freud, Sigmund. The Basic Writings of Sigmund Freud. A. A. Brill, ed. New York: The Modern Library, 1938.

22. Hearn, Gordon. The Process of Group Development. A public lecture given at the University of Toronto under the sponsorship of the School of Graduate Studies and the School of Social Work, December 7, 1955.

23. Hemphill, J. K. A Proposed Theory of Leadership in Small Groups. Columbus: Ohio State University. Personnel Research Board, 1954.

24. James, William. Talks to Teachers on Psychology (1899). Reissued. New York: Henry Holt and Co., 1946.

25. Jennings, H. H. Leadership and Isolation, 2nd ed. New York: Longmans, Green and Co., 1950.

26. Kelly, H. H. and Thibaut, J. W. Handbook of Social Psychology. G. Lindzey, ed., II. Cambridge, Mass.: Addison-Wesley Press, 1954.

27. Knowles, W. H. Personnel Management, a human relations approach. New York: American Book Co., 1955.

28. Kohler, W. Gestalt Psychology. New York: Liveright Pub. Co., 1929.

29. Levine, Jacob and Butler, John. "Lecture vs. Group Decision in Changing Behavior," Journal of Applied Psychology, 36, 1952, pages 29-33.

30. Lewin, Kurt. Resolving Social Conflicts. New York: Harper, 1948.

31. Lewin, Kurt. "Science, Power and Education," Studies in Topological and Vector Psychology, G. W. Lewin, ed., III. 1944.

32. Lewin, Kurt. Field Theory in Social Science. D. Cartwright, ed. New York: Harper, 1951.

33. Lewin, Kurt; Lippitt, R.; and White, R. K. "Patterns of Aggressive Behavior in Experimentally Created Social Climates," Journal of Social Psychology, X, 1939, pages 271-299.

34. Libo, L. Measuring Group Cohesiveness. Ann Arbor: University of Michigan Press, 1953.

35. Lippitt, R. An Experimental Study of the Effect of Democratic and Authoritarian Group Atmospheres. University of Iowa Studies. XVI, No. 3, pages 43-198.

36. Lippitt, R. Current Trends in Social Psychology. Pittsburgh: University of Pittsburgh Press, 1948.

37. Lippitt, R.; Polansky, N.; and Rosen, S. "The Dynamics of Power," Human Relations, V, 1952, pages 37-64.

38. Luft, J. and Ingham, H. The Johari Window, a graphic model for interpersonal relations. Western Training Laboratory in Group Development, August 1955; University of California at Los Angeles, Extension Office. See also: Human Relations Training News. Washington, D. C., National Education Association. V, No. 1, 1961.

39. Mayo, Elton. Human Problems of an Industrial Civilization. New York: Macmillan, 1933.

40. McKeachie, W. J. "The Instructor Faces Automation," Improving College and University Teaching. VIII, No. 3, 1960, pages 91-95.

41. McKeachie, W. J. "Individual Conformity to Attitudes of Classroom Groups," Journal of Abnormal and Social Psychology. 49, 1954, pages 282-289.

42. Moreno, J. L. Psychodrama. New York: Beacon House, 1946.

43. Rodgers, D. The Necessary and Sufficient Criteria of Leadership. Unpublished manuscript.

44. Rogers, Carl. Client Centered Therapy. Boston: Houghton, Mifflin, 1951.

45. Sanford, F. H. "Research on Military Leadership," Psychology in the World Emergency. J. C. Flanagan, ed. Pittsburgh: University of Pittsburgh Press, 1952, pages 17-34.

46. Seeman, M. Leadership in American Education. Chicago: University of Chicago Press, 1950.

47. Sherif, M. The Psychology of Social Norms. New York: Harper, 1936.

48. Sherif, M. "Consistency in Intergroup Relations," Journal of Social Issues, V, No. 3, 1949, pages 32-37.

49. Stock, D. and Luft, J. "T.E.T. Design, a Modification of a T-Group Experience," Training Designs for Human Relations Laboratories. Douglas Bunker, ed. Washington, D. C.: National Education Association, 1962.

50. Tannenbaum, R. and Schmidt, W. H. "How to Choose a Leadership Pattern," Harvard Business Review, March-April 1958.

51. Thelen, H. Dynamics of Groups at Work. Chicago: University of Chicago Press, 1954.

52. World Almanac, H. Hansen, ed. New York: New York World-Telegram and Sun, 1960.

San Fran. Chamber Orchestra
    Jan. 11. Sun. 8:15
       Hillel House, 2736 Bancroft

Group...

Change - to bring about some "significant" change.
    would have to discuss + agree on significance.